Fill My Cup Lord, Let it Overflow With………
By Anthony Russell

Fill My Cup Lord, Let it Overflow With.........

Introduction

There are many times in life that we all need God to fill our cup with all of his bountiful blessings. Every day we require something from God to keep us going throughout the day. It is time for us to be real with God and tell him what we desire. What is it that you stand in the need of on a daily basis to keep you on the right track of not giving up on God? Well today is your day. It is my prayer that when you feel like you are in need of a refill that this book will help you to fill up on God's promised words to all of us. Take a journey with me through the scriptures and let God fill your cup up every day.

All scripture is given by inspiration of God, and is profitable for doctrine, for reproof, for correction, for instruction in righteousness, that the man of God may be complete, thoroughly equipped for every good work. 2 Timothy 3:16.

You search the scriptures, for in them you think you have eternal life; and these are they which testify of Me. John 5:39.

Knowing this first that no prophecy of any private interpretation for prophecy never came by the will of man, but holy men of God spoke as they were moved by the Holy Spirit. 2 Peter 1:21.

Therefore whoever hears these sayings of Mine, and does them, I will liken him to a wise man who built his house on the rock: and the rain descended, the floods came, and the winds blew and beat on that house; and it did not fall, for it was founded on the rock. Matthew 7:24.

Souls in danger, look above, Jesus completely saves, He will lift you by His love out of the angry waves. He's the Master of the sea, billow His will obey; He your Savior wants to be—Be saved today. Love lifted me! Love lifted me! When nothing else could help, Love lifted me!

Fill My Cup Lord, Let It Overflow With Love....

This is My commandment, that you love one another as I have loved you. "Greater love has no one than this, than to lay down one's life for his friends." John 15:12-13.

Finally, all of you be of one mind, having compassion for one another; love as brothers, be tenderhearted, be courteous; not returning evil or reviling for reviling, but on the contrary blessing, knowing that you were called to this, that you may inherit a blessing 1 Peter 3:8-9.

And he has given us this command: Anyone who loves God must also love their brother and sister. 1 John 4:21.

Now that you have purified yourselves by obeying the truth so that you have sincere love for each other, love one another deeply, from the heart. 1 Peter 1:22.

Love does no harm to a neighbor; therefore love is the fulfillment of the law. Romans 13:10.

If I speak in the tongues of men or of angels, but do not have love, I

am only a resounding gong or a clanging cymbal. If I have the gift of

prophecy and can fathom all mysteries and all knowledge, and if I

have a faith that can move mountains, but do not have love, I am

nothing. If I give all I possess to the poor and give over my body to

hardship that I may boast, but do not have love, I gain nothing. Love

is patient, love is kind. It does not envy, it does not boast, it is not

proud. It does not dishonor others, it is not self-seeking, it is not

easily angered, and it keeps no record of wrongs. Love does not

delight in evil but rejoices with the truth. It always protects, always

trusts, always hopes, and always perseveres. Love never fails. But

where there are prophecies, they will cease; where there are

tongues, they will be stilled; where there is knowledge, it will pass

away. For we know in part and we prophesy in part, but when

completeness comes, what is in part disappears. When I was a child,

I talked like a child, I thought like a child, I reasoned like a child.

When I became a man, I put the ways of childhood behind me. For

now we see only a reflection as in a mirror; then we shall see face to

face. Now I know in part; then I shall know fully, even as I am fully known. And now these three remain: faith, hope and love. But the greatest of these is love. 1 Corinthians 13:1-13.

There will be peace in the valley for me some day, there will be peace in the valley for me,
Oh Lord I pray there'll be no sadness, no sorrow, no trouble I see
There will be peace in the valley for me.

Fill My Cup Lord, Let It Overflow With Peace….

"Peace I leave with you; my peace I give you. I do not give to you as the world gives. Do not let your hearts be troubled and do not be afraid." John 14:27.

"Come to me, all you who are weary and burdened, and I will give you rest. Take my yoke upon you and learn from me, for I am gentle and humble in heart, and you will find rest for your souls. For my yoke is easy and my burden is light." Matthew 11:28-30.

"Therefore, since we have been made right in God's sight by faith, we have peace with God because of what Jesus Christ our Lord has done for us." Romans 5:1.

But he was pierced for our transgressions, he was crushed for our iniquities; the punishment that brought us peace was upon him, and by his wounds we are healed. Isaiah 53:5.

You will keep in perfect peace him whose mind is steadfast, because he trusts in you. Isaiah 26:3.

Let the peace of Christ rule in your hearts, since as members of one body you were called to peace. And be thankful. Colossians 3:15.

And the peace of God, which transcends all understanding, will guard your hearts and your minds in Christ Jesus. Philippians 4:7.

The LORD make his face shine upon you and be gracious to you; the LORD turn his face toward you and give you peace." Numbers 6:25-26.

"I have told you these things, so that in me you may have peace. In this world you will have trouble. But take heart! I have overcome the world." John 16:36.

For to be carnally minded is death, but to be spiritually minded is life and peace. Romans 8:6.

Finally, brethren, farewell. Become complete. Be of good comfort, be of one mind, live in peace; and the God of love and peace will be with you. 2 Corinthians 13:11.

Great peace have those who love Your law, and nothing causes them to stumble. Psalm 119:165.

For you shall go out with joy, and be led out with peace; the mountains and the hills shall break forth into singing before you, and all the trees of the field shall clap their hands. Isaiah 55:12.

My chains are gone, I've been set free. My God, my Savior has ransomed me, and like a flood His mercy reigns, unending love, Amazing Grace.

Fill My Cup Lord, Let It Overflow With Forgiveness....

For all have sinned, and come short of the glory of God. Romans 3:23

This, then, is how you should pray: Our Father in heaven, hallowed be your name, your kingdom come, your will be done on earth as it is in heaven. Give us this day our daily bread. Forgive us our debts, as we also have forgiven our debtors, and lead us not into temptation, but deliver us from the evil one. For if you forgive men when they sin against you, your heavenly Father will also forgive you, but if you do not forgive men their sins, your Father will not forgive your sins. Matthew 6:9-15.

And when ye stand praying, forgive, if ye have ought against any: that your Father also which is in heaven may forgive you your trespasses. Mark 11:25

Confess your faults one to another, and pray one for another, that ye may be healed. The effectual fervent prayer of a righteous man availeth much. James 5:16.

But I say unto you which hear, Love your enemies, do good to them which hate you, Bless them that curse you, and pray for them which despitefully use you. Luke 6:27-28.

Forbearing one another, and forgiving one another, if any man have a quarrel against any: even as Christ forgave you, so also do ye. James 5:16.

Judge not, and ye shall not be judged: condemn not, and ye shall not be condemned: forgive, and ye shall be forgiven. Luke 6:37.

If we confess our sins, he is faithful and just to forgive us our sins, and to cleanse us from all unrighteousness. 1 John 1:9.

Bearing with one another, and forgiving one another, if anyone has a complaint against another; even as Christ forgave you, so you also must do. Colossians 3:13.

Therefore if your enemy hungers, feed him; if he thirsts, give him a drink; for in so doing you will heap coals of fire on his head. Do not be overcome by evil, but overcome evil with good. Romans 12:20-21.

Then Peter came to Jesus and asked, "Lord, how many times shall I forgive my brother or sister who sins against me? Up to seven times?" Jesus answered, "I tell you, not seven times, but seventy-seven times. Matthew 18:21-22.

Get rid of all bitterness, rage and anger, brawling and slander, along with every form of malice. Be kind and compassionate to one another, forgiving each other, just as in Christ God forgave you. Ephesians 4:31-32.

My hope is built on nothing less than Jesus' blood and righteousness.
I dare not trust the sweetest frame, but wholly lean on Jesus' name.
On Christ the solid rock I stand,
all other ground is sinking sand; all other ground is sinking sand.

Fill My Cup Lord, Let It Overflow With Hope....

For I know the plans I have for you, declares the LORD, plans for welfare and not for evil, to give you a future and a hope. Jeremiah 29:11

For whatever was written in former days was written for our instruction, that through endurance and through the encouragement of the Scriptures we might have hope. Romans 15:4

When the perishable has been clothed with the imperishable, and the mortal with immortality, then the saying that is written will come true: "Death has been swallowed up in victory. Where, O death, is your victory? Where, O death, is your sting? The sting of death is sin, and the power of sin is law. But thanks be to God! He gives us the victory through our Lord Jesus Christ. Therefore, my dear brothers, stand firm. Let nothing move you. Always give yourselves fully to the work of the Lord, because you know that your labor in the Lord is not in vain. 1 Corinthians 15:54-58.

Joshua said to them, "Do not be afraid; do not be discouraged. Be strong and courageous. This is what the Lord will do to all the enemies you are going to fight." Joshua 10:25.

You will be secure, because there is hope; you will look about you and take your rest in safety. You will lie down with no one to make you afraid, and many will court your favor. Job 11:18-19.

So that being justified by his grace we might become heirs according to the hope of eternal life. Titus 3:7.

For in this hope we were saved. Now hope that is seen is not hope. For who hopes for what he sees? But if we hope for what we do not see, we wait for it with patience. Romans 8:24-25

Through whom also we have obtained our introduction by faith into this grace in which we stand; and we exult in hope of the glory of God. And not only this, but we also exult in our tribulations, knowing that tribulation brings about perseverance; and perseverance, proven character; and proven character, hope; and hope does not disappoint, because the love of God has been poured out within our hearts through the Holy Spirit who was given to us. Romans 5:27.

Jesus said to her, "Everyone who drinks of this water will be thirsty again, but whoever drinks of the water that I will give him will never be thirsty again. The water that I will give him will become in him a spring of water welling up to eternal life." John 4:13-14.

God is not man, that he should lie, or a son of man, that he should change his mind. Has he said, and will he not do it? Or has he spoken, and will he not fulfill it? Numbers 23:19.

Light of the world You stepped down into darkness Opened my eyes let me see
Beauty that made this heart adore You Hope of a life spent with You
Here I am to worship Here I am to bow down
Here I am to say that You're my God

Fill My Cup Lord, Let It Overflow With Praise…

I will bless the Lord at all times; His praise shall continually be in my mouth. Psalm 34:1.

But you are a chosen generation, a royal priesthood, a holy nation. His own special people, that you may proclaim the praises of Him who called you out of darkness into his marvelous light. 1 Peter 2:9.

O praise the LORD, all ye nations: praise him, all ye people. For his merciful kindness is great toward us: and the truth of the Lord endures forever. Praise ye the Lord. Psalm 117:1-2

But thanks be to God, who gives us the victory through our Lord Jesus Christ. 1 Corinthians 15:27.

Great is the LORD, and greatly to be praised. In the city of our God, His holy mountain. Psalms 48:1.

Oh that men would praise the LORD for His goodness, and for His wonderful works to the children of men! Psalm 107:8.

Through Him then, let us continually offer up a sacrifice of praise to God, that is, the fruit of lips that give thanks to His name. Hebrews 13:15.

Praise the Lord! For it is good to sing praises to our God; for it is pleasant and praise is beautiful. Psalm 147:1.

I call upon the LORD, who is worthy to be praised, and I am saved from my enemies. 2 Samuel 22:4.

It is good to give thanks to the LORD and to sing praises to Your name, O Most High; To declare Your lovingkindness in the morning and Your faithfulness by night. Psalm 92:1-2

Then you will say on that day, "I will give thanks to You, O Lord; For although You were angry with me, Your anger is turned away, And You comfort me. Isaiah 12:1.

Praise the LORD! Praise God in His sanctuary; Praise Him in His mighty expanse. Praise Him for His mighty deeds; Praise Him according to His excellent greatness. Psalm 150:1-2.

*Early in the morning, before the break of day, I asked the Lord to
make me whole.
He holds me and the Lord keeps me; oh, joy, joy in my soul.
Joy, joy, God's great joy. Joy, joy, down in my soul;
sweet, beautiful, soul saving joy, oh, joy, joy in my soul.*

Fill My Cup Lord, Let It Overflow With Joy…

Consider it pure joy, my brothers and sisters, whenever you face trials of many kinds, because you know that the testing of your faith produces perseverance. James 1:2-3.

For in the day of trouble he will keep me safe in his dwelling; he will hide me in the shelter of his sacred tent and set me high upon a rock. Then my head will be exalted above the enemies who surround me; at his sacred tent I will sacrifice with shouts of joy; I will sing and make music to the Lord. Hear my voice when I call, Lord; be merciful to me and answer me. Psalm 27:5-7.

Be full of joy in the Lord always. I will say again, be full of joy. Let everyone see that you are gentle and kind. The Lord is coming soon. Philippians 4:4-5.

Jesus said, "The kingdom of heaven is like treasure hidden in a field. When a man found it, he hid it again, and then in his joy went and sold all he had and bought that field." Matthew 13:44.

My lips will shout for joy when I sing praise to you— I whom you have delivered. Psalm 71:23.

For you make me glad by your deeds, Lord; I sing for joy at what your hands have done. How great are your works, Lord, how profound your thoughts! Psalm 92:4-5.

To him who is able to keep you from stumbling and to present you before his glorious presence without fault and with great joy—to the only God our Savior be glory, majesty, power and authority, through Jesus Christ our Lord, before all ages, now and forevermore! Amen. Jude 1:2-5.

For the kingdom of God is not meat and drink; but righteousness, and peace, and joy in the Holy Ghost. Romans 14:17.

Rejoice in the Lord always. I will say it again: Rejoice! Philippians 4:4.

In loving-kindness Jesus came, my soul in mercy to reclaim,
And from the depths of sin and shame, through grace He lifted me.

Fill My Cup Lord, Let It Overflow With Kindness…

Do not let kindness and truth leave you; Bind them around your neck, Write them on the tablet of your heart. Proverbs 3:3.

He has told you, O man, what is good; and what does the Lord require of you but to do justice, to love kindness, And to walk humbly with your God? Micah 6:8.

But when the kindness and love of God our Savior appeared. Titus 3:4

Or do you show contempt for the riches of his kindness, forbearance and patience, not realizing that God's kindness is intended to lead you to repentance? Romans 2:4.

Solomon answered God, "You have shown great kindness to David my father and have made me king in his place." 2 chronicles 1:8.

You gave me life and showed me kindness, and in your providence watched over my spirit. Job 10:12.

May the Lord now show you kindness and faithfulness, and I too will show you the same favor because you have done this. 2 Samuel 2:6.

"Anyone who withholds kindness from a friend forsakes the fear of the Almighty." Job 6:14.

"Now then, please swear to me by the Lord that you will show kindness to my family, because I have shown kindness to you. Give me a sure sign" Joshua 2:12.

I led them with cords of human kindness, with ties of love. To them I was like one who lifts a little child to the cheek, and I bent down to feed them. Hosea 11:4.

But let those who boast boast about this: that they understand and know me, that I am the Lord, who exercises kindness, justice and righteousness on earth, for in these I delight," declares the Lord." Jeremiah 9:24.

In order that in the coming ages he might show the incomparable riches of his grace, expressed in his kindness to us in Christ Jesus. Ephesians 2:7.

Consider therefore the kindness and sternness of God: sternness to those who fell, but kindness to you, provided that you continue in his kindness. Otherwise, you also will be cut off. Romans 11:22.

Faithful, faithful, faithful is our God
Faithful, faithful, faithful is our God
Faithful, faithful, faithful is our God
Faithful, faithful, faithful is our God
I'm reaping the harvest God promised me
Take back what the devil stole from me
And I rejoice today, for I shall recover it all
Yes, I rejoice today, for I shall recover it all

Fill My Cup Lord, Let It Overflow With Faith...

Now faith is the assurance of things hoped for, the conviction of things not seen. Hebrews 11:1.

And without faith it is impossible to please him, for whoever would draw near to God must believe that he exists and that he rewards those who seek him. Hebrews 11:6.

A faithful man will abound with blessings, but whoever hastens to be rich will not go unpunished. Proverbs 28:20.

His master said to him, 'Well done, good and faithful servant. You have been faithful over a little; I will set you over much. Enter into the joy of your master.' Matthew 25:21.

One who is faithful in a very little is also faithful in much, and one who is dishonest in a very little is also dishonest in much. Luke 16:10.

If we are faithless, he remains faithful—for he cannot deny himself. 2 Timothy 2:13.

I have not hidden your deliverance within my heart; I have spoken of your faithfulness and your salvation; I have not concealed your steadfast love and your faithfulness from the great congregation. Psalms 40:10.

But the Lord is faithful. He will establish you and guard you against the evil one. 2 Thessalonians 3:3.

God is faithful, by whom you were called into the fellowship of his Son, Jesus Christ our Lord. 1 Corinthians 1:9.

The steadfast love of the Lord never ceases; his mercies never come to an end; they are new every morning; great is your faithfulness. Lamentations 3:22-23.

Know therefore that the Lord your God is God, the faithful God who keeps covenant and steadfast love with those who love him and keep his commandments, to a thousand generations. Deuteronomy 7:9.

Your steadfast love, O Lord, extends to the heavens, your faithfulness to the clouds. Psalms 36:5.

Who crushed the power of sin and death
My only Savior before the holy Judge
The Lamb who is my righteousness
The Lamb who is my righteousness

Fill My Cup Lord, Let It Overflow With Righteousness...

Finally, brothers and sisters, whatever is true, whatever is noble, whatever is right, whatever is pure, whatever is lovely, whatever is admirable—if anything is excellent or praiseworthy—think about such things. Philippians 4:8.

Whoever pursues righteousness and love finds life, prosperity and honor. Proverbs 21:21.

To do what is right and just is more acceptable to the Lord than sacrifice. Proverbs 21:3.

But seek first his kingdom and his righteousness, and all these things will be given to you as well. Matthew 6:33.

Ill-gotten treasures have no lasting value, but righteousness delivers from death. Proverbs 10:2.

But even if you should suffer for what is right, you are blessed. "Do not fear their threats; do not be frightened." 1 Peter 3:14.

Peacemakers who sow in peace reap a harvest of righteousness.
James 3:18.

Blessed are those who hunger and thirst for righteousness, for they will be filled. Matthew 5:6.

The righteous person may have many troubles, but the Lord delivers him from them all. Psalms 34:19.

Cast your cares on the Lord and he will sustain you; he will never let the righteous be shaken. Psalms 55:22.

But let justice roll on like a river, righteousness like a never-failing stream! Amos 5:24.

The lips of the righteous know what finds favor, but the mouth of the wicked only what is perverse. Proverbs 10:32.

Blessed are those who are persecuted because of righteousness, for theirs is the kingdom of heaven. Matthew 5:10.

Righteousness exalts a nation, but sin condemns any people. Proverbs 14:34.

Better the little that the righteous have than the wealth of many wicked; for the power of the wicked will be broken, but the Lord upholds the righteous. Psalms 37:16-17.

For in the gospel the righteousness of God is revealed—a righteousness that is by faith from first to last, just as it is written: "The righteous will live by faith." Romans 1:17.

Wealth is worthless in the day of wrath, but righteousness delivers from death. Proverbs 11:4.

For he made Him who knew no sin to be sin for us, that we might become the righteousness of God in Him. 2 Corinthians 5:21.

Sweet hour of prayer! Sweet hour of prayer!
That calls me from a world of care,
And bids me at my Father's throne
Make all my wants and wishes known.
In seasons of distress and grief,
My soul has often found relief,
And oft escaped the tempter's snare,
By thy return, sweet hour of prayer!

Fill My Cup Lord, Let It Overflow With Prayer....

"This, then, is how you should pray: 'Our Father in heaven, hallowed be your name, your kingdom come, your will be done on earth as it is in heaven. Give us today our daily bread. And forgive us our debts, as we also have forgiven our debtors. And lead us not into temptation, but deliver us from the evil one.' Matthew 6:9-13.

From my distress I called upon the Lord; The Lord answered me and set me in a large place. The Lord is for me; I will not fear; What can man do to me? The Lord is for me among those who help me. Therefore I will look with satisfaction on those who hate me. It is better to take refuge in the Lord, than to trust in man. Psalms 118:5-8.

Ask, and it will be given to you seek, and you will find; knock, and it will be opened to you. Matthew 7:7.

Praying at all times in the Spirit, with all prayer and supplication. To that end keep alert with all perseverance, making supplication for all the saints. Ephesians 6:18.

"In my distress I called to the Lord, and he answered me. From deep in the realm of the dead I called for help, and you listened to my cry. You hurled me into the depths, into the very heart of the seas, and the currents swirled about me; all your waves and breakers swept over me. I said, 'I have been banished from your sight; yet I will look again toward your holy temple.' The engulfing waters threatened me, the deep surrounded me; seaweed was wrapped around my head. To the roots of the mountains I sank down; the earth beneath barred me in forever. But you, Lord my God, brought my life up from the pit. "When my life was ebbing away, I remembered you, Lord, and my prayer rose to you, to your holy temple. Those who cling to worthless idols turn away from God's love for them. But I, with shouts of grateful praise, will sacrifice to you. What I have vowed I will make good. I will say, 'Salvation comes from the LORD.' Jonah 2:2-9.

And whatever you ask in prayer, you will receive, if you have faith. Matthew 21:22.

"And when you pray, do not heap up empty phrases as the Gentiles do, for they think that they will be heard for their many words. Matthew 6:7.

And this is the confidence that we have toward him, that if we ask anything according to his will he hears us. And if we know that he hears us in whatever we ask, we know that we have the requests that we have asked of him. 1 John 5:14-15.

Is anyone among you sick? Let him call for the elders of the church, and let them pray over him, anointing him with oil in the name of the Lord. And the prayer of faith will save the one who is sick, and the Lord will raise him up. And if he has committed sins, he will be forgiven. Therefore, confess your sins to one another and pray for one another that you may be healed. The prayer of a righteous person has great power as it is working. James 5:14-16.

Never would have made it
Never could have made it without You
I would have lost it all
But now I see how You were there for me

Fill My Cup Lord, Let It Overflow With Perseverance…..

Wait for the Lord; be strong, and let your heart take courage; wait for the Lord! Psalms 27:14.

Rejoice in hope, be patient in tribulation, be constant in prayer. Romans 12:12.

And let us not grow weary of doing good, for in due season we will reap, if we do not give up. Galatians 6:9.

Through him we have also obtained access by faith into this grace in which we stand, and we rejoice in hope of the glory of God. Not only that, but we rejoice in our sufferings, knowing that suffering produces endurance, and endurance produces character, and character produces hope, and hope does not put us to shame, because God's love has been poured into our hearts through the Holy Spirit who has been given to us. Romans 5:2-5.

Blessed is the man who remains steadfast under trial, for when he has stood the test he will receive the crown of life, which God has promised to those who love him. James 1:12.

In all circumstances take up the shield of faith, with which you can extinguish all the flaming darts of the evil one; and take the helmet of salvation, and the sword of the Spirit, which is the word of God, praying at all times in the Spirit, with all prayer and supplication. To that end keep alert with all perseverance, making supplication for all the saints, and also for me, that words may be given to me in opening my mouth boldly to proclaim the mystery of the gospel. Ephesians 6:16-19.

If we endure, we will also reign with him; if we deny him, he also will deny us. 2 Timothy 2:12.

For you have need of endurance, so that when you have done the will of God you may receive what is promised. Hebrews 10:36.

Count it all joy, my brothers, when you meet trials of various kinds, for you know that the testing of your faith produces steadfastness. And let steadfastness have its full effect, that you may be perfect and complete, lacking in nothing. James 1:2-4.

There is a Name I love to hear, I love to sing its worth;
It sounds like music in my ear, The sweetest Name on earth.
Oh, how I love Jesus, Oh, how I love Jesus, Oh, how I love Jesus,
Because He first loved me!

People of God this is what it is about Loving all mankind because God loved us first. God looked beyond our faults and saw our needs and for that we should all say Thank You Lord.. Be Blessed and walk in God's favor over your life..

Love You All….

www.ingramcontent.com/pod-product-compliance
Lightning Source LLC
Chambersburg PA
CBHW030309030426
42337CB00012B/642